MW00768063

Procrastinating Question:
How much time do you invest each day thinking about ways to earn more money?

Action Step:
Ask yourself this daily question: How can I earn more money with the least amount of time and effort?

PROCRASTINATING

LET GO OF THE PAST

and

UNLOCK YOUR FULL POTENTIAL

Timothy K. Moore

PROCRASTINATING
LET GO OF THE PAST AND UNLOCK YOUR FULL POTENTIAL

Copyright © 2018 by Dr. Timothy K. Moore
All rights reserved. This book or any portion thereof may not
be reproduced or used in any manner whatsoever without
the express written permission of the publisher except for
the use of brief quotations in a book review.

Printed in the United States of America
First Printing 2018

Print Book:
ISBN-13: 978-1724678898
ISBN-10: 1724678892

■ ■ ■

Contact Information

support@writingbestsellers.com
gmresourcegroup@gmail.com

Publisher: gmresourcegroup

Link to talk
https://growingyourbusiness.as.me/?appointmentType=3432792

When you're ready for improvement, let's talk!

TABLE OF CONTENTS

ACKNOWLEDGMENTS

Writing an acknowledgment page is fraught with anxiety. You suddenly realize just how many people have helped you get over the finish line and how fallible your memory is. I know I'm going to forget someone who should not be forgotten. If you're that person, my apologies.

Thank you to the following people who have influenced my life in one way or another:

Nettie B. Moore, Tony Robbins, Bob Proctor, Roby Williams, Latanya Moore, Fredia Nelson Womack, Jim Butz, Jackie Towns, Kenneth Wynn, Charla Booth, Dan Sullivan, Lisa Bass, Sanja Lemons, Beverly Johnson, Alan Roman, Alexis Tidwell, Angela Knox, Charles Sim, Joe Polish, Lisa Dunn, Clifton McKnight, Lottie Sims, Corie Johnson, Deborah Henderson, Denise Graham, Vicky Edwards, Charles Thomas, Latricia Arnold, Bill Clinton, John North, Amway, Brenda Generali, Dr. Jane Oelke, Ray Self, T. Allen Hanes, Vickie Shorts, Angeletta Dabney, Les Brown, George Bush, Bobbie Brooks, Sonja Miller, Louisa Smith, Sergio, Cathy Loring, Lonnie Ford, Ronda McKinney Shaw, Fred Jones, Pastor Danny D. Holmes, Dennis Kimbro, Jay Abraham, and Diane Bell.

INTRODUCTION

Every once in a while, people postpone the tasks and assignments they are supposed to perform. Although this is often stressful, delaying a given course of action seldom results in any major psychological suffering. However, for some individuals, deferring what needs to be done can become a persistent behavioral pattern that interferes with daily life. This is referred to as procrastination—that is, voluntarily delaying an intended course of action despite the negative consequences of that delay.

This behavior involves the postponement of initiating or completing a commitment until the last minute, until after a predetermined deadline, or indefinitely. Though similar to the difficulties some individuals face when having to prioritize or when they are being self-assertive, procrastination requires an active choice between competing activities in which one is avoided in favor of the other, and is usually characterized by the preference for an immediate reward or the escape from a potentially adverse experience.

Procrastination is not only associated with negative consequences for the activity being delayed but is also related to decreased well-being, diminished mental health, lower performance, and financial difficulties. In addition, deferring wellness behaviors can often result in treatment delays, a lack of compliance, and the exacerbation of distress, most notably with reference to physical illness.

Procrastination is not merely a curious human aberration. It is one of the many instances in which people fail to pursue their interests in an efficient and productive manner. It represents a dysfunction of the human abilities that are important, if not essential, for coping with myriad tasks, major or minor, that accumulate daily on our desks, in our memo books, or in our minds. When we procrastinate, we waste time, miss opportunities, and do not live authentic lives.

This book is for those individuals who are tired of procrastinating and want to be able to make decisions, take control of their lives, and do the things they know they ought to be doing to make a change and have direction so as to be more comfortable and excited about their lives.

My hope is that you will walk away with a newfound understanding of the many facets of procrastination. Everyone procrastinates—there's no perfect individual!—but we must put procrastination in its place so that we are not putting off those things that we must accomplish today!

CHAPTER 1

BELIEVE THE CHANGE BEFORE YOU SEE IT

The world as we have created it is a process of our thinking. It cannot be changed without changing our thinking.

— Albert Einstein

We're talking about procrastinating. Why are we afraid to succeed? Why is this book about procrastination and not something else? In the world we live in today, people procrastinate more than you might imagine. There's always a reason for us not doing those things we know we ought to be doing. We're delayed, we put things off, and we don't feel comfortable about doing them. There are a million reasons why we don't do the things that we should be doing.

Everybody procrastinates in some form or fashion but the majority of us don't realize how much we procrastinate or stop things that we should be doing more of. Procrastinating is not something that's comfortable yet we still do it. We put off tomorrow's stuff. We put off today's stuff. We make excuses for why we cannot accomplish a task.

This book is not for those who have books about procrastination and are doing nothing with them. This book is about doing the things that you need to do to stop procrastination, improve your life, and better your outcome.

Procrastinating stops us from doing the things that should be planned out or set in stone to accomplish.

Why do we procrastinate? Why do we put off things that we can do now? Why do certain tasks seem so impossible that we can't take control of them and do the things that are easy and not complicated?

When it comes to procrastination, I think about my own story; how I had a major issue with my health because I kept delaying something that I knew was going on. And the thing about it is, it cost me my leg, up to my knee. I had a blister on my foot from doing Zumba twice a day. I was exercising and I knew I had broken the skin on my foot. I thought it would heal by itself so I did not seek medical attention.

Lo and behold, it turned into a fever and it turned into an infection, and next thing you know, I found myself in front of some doctors feeling uncomfortable about what they were telling me. The infection had traveled through my leg to give me a systemic infection. I procrastinated. I kept thinking, *Oh, I've got this. I can take some over-the-counter things. I can just deal with it because it's not that bad. I've had a blister on my foot before.*

And you know, we go through life and we don't worry about those blisters and those little cuts and the little scratches, not thinking that they mean much, but mine was a major issue because before I realized it, I had a traumatic fever. I was always cold and always hot. I couldn't shake this. I couldn't figure it out.

Now, I knew a lot about medical stuff but I was like, *Why is this happening?* I remember checking myself into the hospital. I went to the emergency room, and they thought, *What are you doing?* When they got my lab results and my white blood cell count was off the charts, they knew I was in trouble. I didn't think about it. I just figured, like many of you might, oh, give me a pill, give me an aspirin, give me something simple, and we can all go about our business. Well, my issue was not that simple. Long story short, I wound up getting my leg amputated—from procrastinating.

I'm not saying your situation is that dramatic. But I procrastinated and put off my own health. What are you putting off today that you need to change in your life? That thing that, if you don't take care of it, is going to cause you heartache, pain, misery, or discomfort? Maybe it won't result in something as severe as getting your leg amputated but you know what? Procrastinating cost me my leg and by putting things off, it cost me a lot of other things as well.

One thing we all need to do is just stop. Stop. What are you doing right now? Stop and decide what you're going to change about your life. What is it about your life that is not important that is stopping you from having the life you want to have?

Let's talk about your goals. What is your number-one goal right now? What's the goal you've been putting off? Now, I'm not talking about something like buying a car or a house, or something that you've done before. I'm talking about a goal that, if you don't reach it, you know you're going to feel pain. And I want you to feel the pain because you haven't attained that goal. I want you to feel the pain because you know the importance of this goal. What is it that's holding you back? Who are you afraid of? Think about it. What is holding you back when you think about your goals?

Now, you are what you think about all day long. What is it that you think about all day? What is it that, when you come to your office or you go to your home office, or you go to work, or you plan out your day, will make you not plan your goals? Think about it. What is it? All this has to do with decisions and decisions lead to procrastinating. What are you putting off? Why is it so hard to make an immediate decision and tell someone, "No, I have to focus on a situation that I'm involved in right now."

In this book, we're going to talk about many ways to enhance and improve your life, to give you back those things that you thought were impossible to have. Who's stopping you from doing those things? What's stopping you? Are you in the same position you were a year ago? Ask yourself that question. Are your finances the same way? Is your life the same way? What has improved in your life from a year ago today? Are your finances where you really want them to be? Do you know your finances are where they are because of where you are today? Have you done anything? Do you make goals?

What did you do today? As you're reading this book right now, what did you plan for today? What are the three personal goals you plan to reach today? What are the three business goals you plan to reach today?

Stop. Don't read any more. What are you going to do? Put off those phone calls that are not important. What are you going to do *today* that's going to generate revenue? Do you know how to generate revenue? That's the question. Do you know how...or are you afraid to?

The concepts in this book are simple. There are going to be challenges. This material is going to raise questions for you. It's going to give you answers but it's also going to help better you all the way around. You're going to do a 180, and the 180 will turn into a 360-degree revenue increase, allowing you to be happy and live the life that you want to live.

I'm going to ask you a question. Are you the person you want to be? Are you the individual you want to be? When you look at your life today, is it where you want it to be? What about making changes? What about changes that you have to make today—not tomorrow, today! Not in a couple of hours but right now! Have you put a sign on your door telling everybody to stay away? Block them out for 90 minutes while you work some things out. Have you turned off the phone? Have you turned off the computer? Have you just thought about that project that was due three weeks ago...the one that's still sitting in your cubicle?

This book is about changing your life. This book is about challenging yourself. This book is about doing those things that are uncomfortable that you should have done. It will help you become the person that you want to become. What are you going to do?

Go back. Stop. I want you to write about the individual that you want to become, that you envision yourself as in business and in your personal life. Write it out. Think about it. Spend some time with it. Are you where you want to be today?

Your Thoughts

CHAPTER 2

WHY DO MY DECISIONS AFFECT MY PROCRASTINATION?

Nobody's life is ever all balanced. It's a conscious decision to choose your priorities every day.

— Elisabeth Hasselbeck

There is an old saying that goes like this: "He who hesitates is lost." She who hesitates is lost. No good thing comes out of delay, hesitation, and putting things off for tomorrow. These are habits. These are things we often ask ourselves when we think about things — and I ask questions myself, such as: Why do my decisions affect my procrastination?

Decisions have a lot to do with procrastination. Just ask yourself...can you make a decision without asking someone else their opinion? Can you make a decision that's going to help your business grow 10-plus or 100-fold? Can you make a decision without thinking about what someone else is going to say about your decision? And then, can you make a decision that's going to make you happy?

Decision. It's a take-charge word. When you take charge of your decisions, when you take action *now*, you're actually going to be better off if you go ahead and make that gut decision without worrying about the outcome...because you already know the outcome. You already know what's going to happen. But the word "decision" bogs us down with fear. Then we're not able to go further in life or deal with our projects or the people around us, or we're just stuck. *Decision* is an everyday part of our lives, from the time we get up to the time we go to rest. From the time you wake up your children to the time you go to school, everything around your life is influenced by some type of decision that you have to make. And nobody can make your decisions but you.

There was an interesting study done about decisions. They brought in two groups of people to complete a project and the project was laid out before them. The first group came in. There were six people in this group. And the six people in this group were given eight things they needed to decide on in a week's time. That's six people, eight things to decide on, and make a decision in one week.

Then they brought the other group in, and the other group only had three people but they had two things they had to decide on. But they had to decide on them *now*. Not next week, not tomorrow, but today.

It's interesting when you look at it. Eight people had six items they had to consider and make a decision about in one week's time. The second group was three in number and they had to make a decision today. Not tomorrow, not next week. Today.

When they brought them all back together, it was really interesting how things turned out. The people that had one day to decide on the two issues were extremely happy with their decisions. They'd made the decisions right then, immediately. And they were completely satisfied with their decisions.

The six people who had eight decisions to make were totally uncomfortable with what they chose. They had a whole week to plan things out but they were miserable.

A lot of times when there's a decision we have to make, we need to take advantage of the opportunity because it's happening *now*. The body is able to deal with whatever you're dealing with. The six test subjects were able to focus on things that were presented to them but had too much time to think about them. The three people didn't rationalize. They thought about it immediately and they came up with the best decisions. And guess what? The three people were really happy with their decisions, while the six were not.

Are you happy with your decisions? Do you put off your decisions or do you make hurried decisions? What do you do? When you think about it, individuals who are truly happy are quick decision makers. And they make adaptations effortlessly. They have no problem.

Those living in fear — or as I say, with an upset stomach or having a headache or not making decisions — aren't able to make a decision in the moment. What decisions are you afraid to make now?

It's amazing. When we're disciplining children we can sometimes make a decision at the moment. Just imagine if you had to tell your child, who was doing something at school that you didn't appreciate, "Okay, I'll give you five days to think about what you did and how we're going to punish you."

Other parents will do whatever they want to do right away.

Some parents can do it now and some people will go back on their decisions. What's your stance?

One of the things I always talk about is to start making decisions *now*, on the fly, at the moment. Yeah, you're going to be a little uncomfortable because it's not going to seem like you, but when you look at what you have accomplished at the end of the day, you'll see that those "right now" decisions are life-changing. They free you up for the things you really want to do and accomplish—things you don't have to put off; things you have to do now because you are the captain of your ship. If the ship has no captain, it has no direction. But when you make that decision to do what you need to do, fear is not an issue anymore because you're standing there proud of what you have decided to do—and proud that it has been accomplished!

Have you ever thought about what people who have really accomplished things in their lives are ecstatic about and have done really well? They were able to make decisions on the fly, at the moment, and research has shown that if you're able to do that, life is much better. Because if we keep delaying things, they become a problem. An issue. A pain. A disappointment. A guilt.

You have to consider whether you are going to be happy with your decision or whether you are going to let your decisions turn into fear. And fear robs us of so much of the greatness that we're trying to achieve in life.

Fear has taken over, so what are you going to do? Are you going to make the decision now? Or are you going to think about it, and let fear make you overthink it and cause you to be confused or afraid?

Or are you going to do what research shows is the way to avoid procrastination — make the decision now and be happy? Just think about it. And the next time you have something to do, *act*. Do it now. Don't think about it. Make it happen at this moment. Just do it!

The question to ask yourself is...why? Why did I give up my power? Why did I let decisions run into procrastination to the degree that I can't say yes or no? Why? Keep asking yourself, why do I keep putting off things that I could do today? Why did I not believe what was before me? Why do I not want to go to the gym? Why do I not want a bigger paycheck? Why do I not want to take more vacations? Why do I not want to relax and meditate more? Why did I not want to read more? Why?

All of these are decisions that prevent us from procrastinating and not doing those things that we should be doing.

That's why we act. But we have to get back to that point and say, "I'm going to do it. I'm going to make the decision. I'm going to make the decision for me."

It's amazing how we allow other people to come into our lives and transform who we are to who they are. Who's going to walk before you? It's amazing. You can walk the same walk with somebody else but one of you is going to take the lead. Who's going to take the lead in your life? Why can't *you* take the lead?

There I go again! Why can't you take the lead and do the things you want to do to transform your life? Do you ask yourself what the reason might be? Why do we talk about why our decisions make us procrastinate? Why? After all, you're in control! No one is making decisions for you, so why are you allowing those decisions to cause you to procrastinate?

What do you want? What was your dream when you sat down and started doing the things that you're doing today? You've probably done a lot to get to this point in your life. But what was your dream?

Number one, what would you say you were going to do? And then, what did you say you weren't going to allow somebody to do to you? And then, why did you allow them to do the things they were doing to you? Because...why? Why? Ask yourself, why? Why can't I make the right decision or why can't I make decisions, period? Or...why do I keep putting off the decisions that I can make now? And why do my decisions seem to hurt me financially, mentally, physically, and emotionally? Why?

Can you answer those questions? I often ask my clients, who is your Superman? What is your kryptonite? Who's stopping you from getting what you want in life? A lot of us are right at our breakthrough point but we don't realize that it is right in front of us. But the decision lies in our hands. We must also open our hands and make sure that no one is controlling our decisions, which leads to more procrastinating.

Are you ready to change what you're doing? Are you ready to live the life that you want to live? You can be more than you are today but first, you have to understand that procrastination is not the controlling factor in your life. And procrastination does not control your decisions — your decisions control procrastination. You have to want to do those things — decide to do them — and change them now. Not tomorrow, not next week, not "I'll think about it."

Maybe you should wake up in the morning and think about it because when you look at your life and look back at what's been going on, you can look in the mirror and say, "What is wrong with me today? Why am I stumbling? Why am I stopping? Why am I not doing the things that I know are going to benefit me in my life and make me happy, as well as my clients and my friends?"

Who has that much power over you? Remove them from your life. Get them away from you. As the old folks used to say, handle them with a long-handled spoon. Refuse to be affected by their power and as a result, you will regain your own power and be able to make decisions *now*. You have to look at certain aspects of your life because when it comes to procrastinating, you need to ascertain what is causing this behavior. Decisions, fear...what is it? Why do you procrastinate?

We talked about it earlier. Stress. It's one of the issues. It's a major component. When we're stressed from work, relationships, friendships, not having enough money — whatever's going on in your life — it causes us to procrastinate. We get cozy in a chair and we eat some Ben and Jerry's ice cream, or we might get our favorite pizza or our favorite Chinese dish. Whatever it might be, we sit there and we put off those things that we need to be accomplishing now.

So, when you think about it, you might be on the internet. You might be texting. You might be on the phone. But stress leads to procrastination. And that's why a lot of times when we look at the decisions we need to make, we put them off. They're not important at the moment anymore because we are finding distractions. So we procrastinate.

It's amazing how it can boomerang and cause us to fear something. Stressful situations pop up because of what we *should have* done. Projects should have been completed and finalized but we have allowed stress to prevent us from making a decision, so we procrastinate and put off those things that we need to be getting done.

It doesn't matter. We all have those challenges. We all go through those "coulda, woulda, shoulda" situations. But you're human, just like everybody else. So it's time to get off your butt. It's time to make the decision that you're going to do these things that will benefit you and your family. Something that's going to change you for the better!

We've got to do things in this life that are sometimes uncomfortable. Can we beat procrastination? Yes. Is it going to be gone forever? No. Because we're always going to have stressful situations in our lives that we must face.

Stress has been around since the beginning of time and it's never going away. But you can control stress and you can control decisions that lead to fear. So, think about it. What's stressing you out at this moment, that's causing you to put off projects or decision-making about things you need to accomplish today?

Write them down. Put them on a sheet of paper. Make a goal — one, two, and three. No more than one, two, and three. Then write down the date and time when you need to get them done. Today, tomorrow, next week....whatever. But put them in order of importance and don't let anything stop you from accomplishing these goals today.

Your Thoughts

CHAPTER 3

CAN PROCRASTINATION BE CURED?

There will always be a million reasons to wait until later. This is simply the nature of the animal called life.

— Richie Norton

C an you cure procrastination? That's the question I'm always asked. Can it be cured? I know I'm slow. I know I don't do things like most people but what stops me when I want to do the things that I *need* to do?

When you learn about procrastinating you'll find that most high achievers delay. You're not alone when you are procrastinating and feel like you can't go on. We have to determine whether procrastination can be cured or whether it is just a part of our daily lives.

Everybody procrastinates. If you think about it for a second, remember when you were going to school and you had term papers that were due or school projects that were due — it happens even in high school and beyond — and how you would put things off until the last moment before doing them? Now, the funny thing about it is, we have so much urgency when we're trying to get things done at the last minute, even though they are past due. The importance of the emergence of the situation means that we *must* do this *now* to get it accomplished, even if it includes late-night sessions, all-night sessions, and we don't sleep at all until we get the project done.

It all comes down to our original question: Can you cure procrastination? Well, one thing about procrastinating is, we procrastinate even though we know we need to do something. We put off going to the doctor. We know we need to go but we keep putting it off. We delay going to the dentist. We procrastinate about doing household chores. There are things we know we need to do but we put them off. When we look around, we find almost endless ways to put off things that could have been done today.

I mean, due to procrastination, you delay a lot of things you want to do and you keep postponing them. When you think about procrastination, you realize that it affects many different things in your life, and a lot of those things are quite touching. Procrastination causes stress.

I've got to get it done.

Oh, am I going to get it done?

What if I don't get it done?

We are procrastinating that way and it leads to stress, and it causes all kinds of issues with our bodies.

Anxiety is also one of the results of procrastination. We know we've got to get it done but we keep putting off those little tasks that soon become big mountains. Can you relate to that? Has it ever happened to you? Have you ever put off something that you know was small but it later became huge? As an example, you know there's a nail in your tire and it has a slow leak. Every day you put a little air into your tire to offset the slow leak. But one day, it becomes an emergency because now the tire is flat. It was a small issue at first and you procrastinated, delayed it until it became a severe issue that you could not escape. We procrastinate and we feel guilty. We feel guilty about the things that we know we need to do. We're embarrassed. We're upset with ourselves sometimes. We have temper tantrums and we're like, why do I keep putting that off? There's nothing like having guilt and it messes with you tremendously.

Some of us have panic attacks. It's like the fire truck is coming and we can't stop. Are you guilty of the fire-truck attack? We panic for reasons that we don't have to and because we procrastinate. We keep putting these issues and tasks off that we need to get done *today*, not tomorrow, not next week. We need to get them done today so that we can regain control of our lives.

Now, we have projects all the time. We have trips we need to go on and we have dates we want to go on. We procrastinate about our marriages and we procrastinate about so many things that we want to do. We find a way to make an excuse and excuses cause us all kinds of turmoil. There are also health problems. We know we've got an issue going on, we know we've got a tooth that needs to be pulled. We know we've got a slight headache. We know we need to get our annual checkup or our six-month checkup but we put them off. We procrastinate until it becomes an issue, then we find ourselves in a place in life where we didn't realize we had become that ill. We put off our problems and also our productivity.

Productivity. I don't know if you have ever been accused of a lack of productivity or laziness. Oh, I have. We drag a project on that could be paying us today or could benefit us in some way. We realize we have the time to do it but we procrastinate and delay it. And in delaying it, it causes us problems and becomes an emergency. Oh, *now* it's an emergency! I've got to get this project done!

I don't think you can ever cure procrastination but you can improve your tendencies toward procrastination to live a more balanced life. We're happy to prioritize certain things and put a start date and an end date on them. When we do that, we can see what we need to do, how we can change our lives, and how we can change the things that are presented to us every day.

Everybody procrastinates, I don't care who they are. From the CEO to the janitor, from the ballplayer to the basketball coach, from the person going to daycare to the employee at that daycare, to the person who's doing nothing — everybody procrastinates.

Imagine that someone doesn't have a job, yet he or she procrastinates. They're looking for a job but they're delaying because they say, "I've got time."

When you start talking about a cure, the cure is simply that we have to plan out our days and nights. We have to plan them and live by our expectations. Now, there are always going to be emergencies that come up that are going to take us out of our plan of action but we have to jump back on the horse.

It's almost like going on a diet. You go on a diet and you know you shouldn't be eating a particular thing on the menu. The question is, do you eat it or not?

Well, some people could eat it and jump back on the plan, and some people could eat it and feel so guilty afterward, they don't want to get back on the program. We must start again on the plan. It's like the ants in the road. The ants are like us. The ants are on a mission but when there is an issue in the way, the ants learn how to go around, tweak the issue, and regain their formation.

When you lose function, you need to restore your function and start over, but keep yourself straight so you can do the things you want to do.

Can procrastination be cured? Can I get my life back? Can I get more balance? Yes but you've got to include procrastination in the balance. Every time you allow someone to come into your atmosphere, your world, or your psyche and interrupt you from a phone call, from a text message, from an email, or a project, it takes you an average of 11 minutes to get back on track every time you're interrupted. What is your time worth?

When it comes to curing procrastination, I'm going to leave you with this: What is your time worth? Who are you allowing to cause you to procrastinate, to cost you your time with your family, loss of income, or loss of productivity? What's important?

Look at your calendar. Look at what you put off from two days ago, the day before, and today. Look at where you are today and see if it's worth it. How much did it cost you? How much is your time worth each day? Have you ever calculated what you're worth and what procrastination costs you in a day? Just think about it. We have 2,000 hours a year that we can work on average but we have 8,000 hours total. When you break it down, from the time you sleep to the time you wake up, we have over 4,000 hours in which we can do anything we want to do.

When you think about procrastinating and time wasted, how much does it cost you? Put the pencil on the paper and see if that interruption for a cup of coffee, for looking at your cell phone, taking a text, and for looking at that email is worth what it is costing you. Take your time and look at it and you will be astonished at what that time is worth. Now, can you write it off? That's up to you but I doubt it because lost time is not regained.

We all have the same 24 hours in a day. So...can procrastination be cured? Not like you think but it can be controlled, and it should be because the bottom line is, it is the key to your future, your success, and the things you want to do in life. If someone wants to interrupt you, put a note up that reads "do not disturb" for 90-minute increments. These 90-minute increments equal almost three hours of work time. Can you imagine what those hours are worth in money to you? When you figure out what your monetary worth per hour is, per second, per minute, you will realize that someone stopping by to chat is not worth it unless they're scheduled in.

Remember, can it be *cured*? No. It can be *controlled*. Whether you succeed is up to you. Follow the steps.

Your Thoughts

CHAPTER 4

ENTREPRENEURSHIP

The entrepreneur is essentially a visualizer and actualizer. He can visualize something, and when he visualizes it he sees exactly how to make it happen.

— Robert L. Schwartz

As entrepreneurs, we must understand that failure is okay. If we don't fail in life, in projects, or in relationships, we can't improve. You might ask yourself, "Why does this have anything to do with procrastination?" Because if you look at your life and look at situations in your life, you'll see that you have procrastinated and have stopped doing things that you thought you should be doing. Even though they are important, we tend to put things off that we feel will be taken care of in time.

But as an entrepreneur, a self-employed business owner, regardless of what your task is, there are going to be issues. We're going to have problems, setbacks, and we're going to have dilemmas. We're going to face things that are going to be uncomfortable. Sit back and look at your life, at what you're doing. Sometimes it seems hard to take constructive criticism from someone in your surroundings. But a lot of times it's all right to fail. It's okay not to get it right. It's okay not to know everything about a project. It's okay to let someone else come in and help out.

We might feel that they're second-guessing us when they offer to help. Well, they're not second-guessing us, they're our eyes and ears to an issue or problem that sometimes we don't see. We wonder why we procrastinate, why we just won't do something. As we do things and we lay the groundwork to do them, sometimes we have to ask the question: Why do I delay dealing with an issue that's going on right now? It's almost like a question you ask yourself every day. Am I doing the best job I can do? Now, when you ask yourself that question, you can't blame anybody else for the result if you're not.

We have to understand that we're going to have problems. We're going to have setbacks. We make goals. We make dreams, and we look at our thoughts and our goals but sometimes, we don't look at them intensively to see what we have laid out for ourselves. And a lot of the goals we set for ourselves are too far-fetched. They're drawn out too far in the future. But if we stop and say, "What is the number-one thing I need to accomplish today? Number two? Number three..." what typically happens? We accomplish those goals! We assign urgency to them.

It's almost like you're sitting in a room waiting to see if somebody is going to give you a project. What talent sells? Listening sells, and sometimes we don't listen enough to understand what the customer asked so we procrastinate, and we put it off, and we say, "Maybe it's not for me. Maybe they want some bigger firm or some smaller firm." When that procrastination leads to a delay, a lot of times it's not that they're looking for a bigger company but simply that they're looking for someone who listens and understands them. As we procrastinate, we put things off. We know we need to answer but the answer or our choice is delayed, which goes back to the question of why we delay something out of fear that's going to benefit us. Why do we allow fear to stop us from doing those things that we know we need to do until they become urgent? After all, once seriousness kicks in, a sense of emergency kicks in and we jump on the issue at hand.

But we have to understand what the reason for the fear is. We go through life and we live in different ways, and we've got things going on but we stop. I challenge you to ask yourself, what makes you happy in what you're doing now? Put your pen down. Stop typing. What makes you happy doing what you're doing now?

Are you happy with what you're doing? Because a lot of times, we wake up with a goal in mind but we don't write it out. It might be at the forefront of your mind but you need to stop and build a dialogue of what you're going to do each day and live by it.

Now, I know...we live by computers. But sometimes with your dialogue you need to write these things out on a sheet of paper and pin them to your computer or to your wall or your desk — wherever you can see them every day. That way, you're able to make a sound judgment regarding the things you need to accomplish.

A lot of times we don't do this because we sit and wait until... And then things go back to that emergency state of being.

I always ask entrepreneurs, "What makes you happy?" And you have to understand that a lot of times, our procrastination leads us away from other things that we want to do.

Now, it's all right if you find yourself sometimes not satisfied with what you're doing at the moment. It's time for a timeout. Stop what you're doing and do something else to get your mind back to where it needs to be. What I mean by that is, wash your car. Go to a movie. Sit and have a cup of coffee, watch a movie at home. Do something that takes your mind off what you're procrastinating about and allow yourself to dream. Allow yourself to have visions and to do something different. And then when you come back, start your project all over again. But only when you're ready to start.

What we have to do as entrepreneurs is handle distractions. One of the best ways I have found to handle distractions is with my 90-minute close-out sessions. No one gets in my space during these sessions. I like to do things in 90-minute increments. That way, I have no distractions and can accomplish the things that I need to do.

What is it that's holding you back? I don't think anything is holding you back. I think sometimes it's simply direction. It's direction on where I'm going, and as entrepreneurs, we sometimes get caught up in the know-it-all syndrome. I know it all, so who can tell me? That's where mentors come in. That's where coaches come in. That's why someone who's been where you are can talk to you and guide you so that you don't make the same mistakes.

We're going to make mistakes. We're going to have issues. We're going to have headaches. But only we can control things and change those things when they come up. That's why a lot of times you hear the saying "less is more." A lot of times, it is.

Put yourself in a circle of people who understand what you're doing. Now, is everybody in the circle going to get along? No, but we also talk about behavior — the behaviors and circumstances around that circle of influence. What is their behavior like? Are their dreams and aspirations like yours? Do they believe in what you're doing? Or are you hanging around negativity all day long trying to accomplish the things you're trying to achieve? A lot of times, negativity will impair our decisions regarding the things we're trying to do. For you to make the proper decision, ask yourself, "What's important?"

When you're procrastinating, just let it go...a little game I play called *creativity*. Creativity takes me from my present situation to a new position. It allows me to create something around what I'm working on. Maybe your project is working on a website. Maybe it's putting a proposal together. Perhaps it's deciding on a speaking engagement. Put creativity around you and ask yourself, "How would I accomplish this if I..." What would you do differently? Because while your words, your dreams, or what you are trying to accomplish for your client are all highly significant, you have to be happy in what you're doing in order to deliver to them.

Are they going to pay you? Is it free for you? Are you just doing some consulting work? What is it? I mean, it doesn't matter. We live in a world where we worry about what someone's going to say about us, how they talk about us, how their opinion matters to us but the bottom line is, it shouldn't matter. Because it's about you.

We understand that we are servers, that we work for other people and we do the best job we can for the customer, but we know that there will always be critics. We're going to always have people who don't believe us and don't want to be around us. Well, that's all right! It's okay to be by yourself sometimes because when you think about it, we live in a world where we're always looking at what's going on. Our time is eaten up by our phones, computers, tablets, and people interrupting us. If you think about it for a second, you'll see that we spend time watching celebrities who don't care about us, football players who don't care about us, and events that don't benefit us. We waste a lot of productive time that we could have put into more productive activities to improve our lives.

So, when you look at your life, look at it as though it is starting now and you're in control. Take control of your life and stop allowing those time stealers to control your life because, in the end, it's about you. You and your family. What makes you happy? What do you want to do? What makes you sad? If you could change something in your life today, something that could lessen your habit of procrastinating, what would you change? When you look at it, you will realize that you have a lot to improve upon.

It's not just procrastination, it's that as entrepreneurs, we are reliant upon our customers. How do we do things to make them happy? We rely on what they want. We say we'll get back to them but we only get back to them when it becomes an emergency.

However, if you live by your goals, dreams, and aspirations, and you live by the things that you want to accomplish *today*, learn to relax and enjoy what you're doing and how you're doing it, then you must understand that procrastination is part of life. It's always going to be with us, regardless of what we're doing, from the time we're born to the present. It has always been an issue and procrastination leads to fear and indecisiveness.

Why do we delay making a decision that we need to make now? Why? What is it about that decision that makes our stomach hurt? Gives us a headache? Causes us to have blurred vision? Wants us to go to sleep, wants us to get away, and wants us to have an attitude? What is it about procrastination and decision that leads to fear?

It helps if we understand the word "fear." It's just four letters, F-E-A-R. Fear has no life. Fear has no ruling in your life. We must learn to control it because there is no such thing as fear when it comes to life. We put it there because of indecision. We are afraid of how we might appear to others, to our peers. Don't worry about them. We're always going to have peers and people who don't like what we say or do. But nonetheless, we must move ahead to accomplish the goals we have set forth.

Well, what do we need to change? Just ourselves. And look at what you have to see! When you are at work, look at your outcome at the end of the day. Look at your results coming back in. Start at the end and come forward with it. Watch how you took on and changed all the dilemmas and the things that you had planned. And as you look at your situation, imagine it being accomplished.

What does that look like, the projects you're doing for yourself or the projects you're doing for others? What does it look like when they are accomplished and done? We have to look at it that way because we get tied up, tangled up, confused, and upset when things don't go the way they're supposed to. A lot of times, it goes the way it does because we set it in motion that way. We don't imagine it going any other way and we look at our life and say, "Who do I blame?"

Go back to that mirror and look into it. We all have the same 24 hours. Whether we make things successful depends on how we use those 24 hours. But not only to us — we must rely on what we want our customers to appreciate as well. You might be saying, "I don't want to delay. I want to get better. But why do I delay?"

Quit asking yourself that. Just make a plan of action. That way, you don't procrastinate as much because if you are thinking, you're going to delay and slow your progress. If we can't make decisions or are afraid of our accomplishments, we're not going to take action. Why are we afraid to make money? What is it about making money? What is it about procrastinating that leads us to think that if we get ahead, we're only going to fail?

It's not about that. When you accomplish a goal, celebrate. Don't worry about whether something will happen. Learn to celebrate any little accomplishment at that moment without worrying about the future. Take it out of your mind. Quit thinking about the negative that you think will happen when you accomplish a goal.

Congratulations! Procrastination is not an issue. The issue is what you want to do today that you didn't do yesterday. What are you going to do today that you can't leave until tomorrow? When will you quit focusing on the past? Live today as today. Don't worry about what happened yesterday. Look at the future and learn to relax and love who you are, love what you're doing, and take control of your life.

Your Thoughts

CHAPTER 5

CRITICAL ABANDONMENT

AND HOW IT AFFECTS OUR LIVES

Many times, though, when people feel as if The Universe has abandoned them, the truth is that they have abandoned their dreams, and as a result they have abandoned The Universe. What we think is being done TO US, we are actually doing TO ourselves. It's a totally crazy reversal that is true most of the time.

— Mastin Kipp

C ritical abandonment stops us from doing things that, when we really think about it, we need to do in our everyday lives. Critical abandonment makes us focus on the things that stop us from success, the things that confuse our lives, and takes our focus away from the things we're trying to accomplish.

When you look at the term "critical abandonment," it might seem like a funny term to use. Critical abandonment is defined as when we are not able to let go of items or individuals that are causing us grief. When you think about procrastinating and how we put things off because of indecision, you realize how indecision can cause us to have fear. When I look at the term "critical abandonment" and how things around us affect us in so many ways, I realize how it, somewhat incredibly, makes things that don't matter, matter. Things that don't matter enhance how we sabotage our lives. They stop us from doing a lot of things that we want to do and that we feel good about doing. But when you stop and you analyze those circumstances or those situations, you suddenly begin to realize that a lot of those imperfections, a lot of those roadblocks, a lot of those obstacles, should be removed, deleted, eliminated, and buried because they are causing health issues, production issues, or anger issues. They're causing so many issues that when we look at our lives, we don't understand how we're going to change those issues. And so, when we look at our lives, our businesses, and our careers, we tend to blame someone else for where we are in life.

A lot of times, we look at who we should blame or who is responsible for our character or actions as they're laid out in front of us. I'm often asked, who should I blame? And I say look in the mirror. The blame starts in the mirror. Because as we go through life, we're taught to hold on to things, whether positive or negative, and not let them go. We continue to process them and hold on to them, thinking that eventually, things are going to untangle and unweave themselves.

In our lives, it's amazing when you look at day-to-day things and you wonder, how did I get to this point? How did it get critical? How did it get to the point where the needle, instead of being green, is now red? And it's buzzing past red, the top is about to explode, and the rubber is coming off. The area itself is becoming contaminated, hot, spoiled, and dangerous. But we've allowed these critical situations and abandonment. We look at our lives and we wonder why we're stressed about so many little things. When you analyze those little particles, those little issues, they amount to very little. But because we can't decide to eliminate and remove the distractions, the distractions now become like a sore. You knew it was going to get infected but you kept picking at it and it got infected to a point that now it's a critical issue. So when you take a critical issue, or critical abandonment sabotage, and you look at it, what do we need to do to eliminate the sabotage or the saboteur who is causing the problem?

Is it easy? It depends on how you look at the saboteur. It's like housing and our homes. Whatever your age is now, at a certain point in life, you'll be over 40. And if you look at the things in your life and your home that you've accumulated, there are clothes that you've had since high school that you'll never, ever put on again. That's considered a critical abandonment that we won't let go of. These are the things that we have to remove, let go of, abandon. There are relationships that we have to remove, let go of, and abandon because a lot of times, you go back to the saboteur or sabotaging behavior and wonder why you're stuck at a certain point in your life and can't move any further. This is because of those saboteurs that we have allowed to affect our lives.

Saboteurs are only a problem when we open the door to allow them in. It often happens when I talk about marriage and people wonder why their relationship is not working. Well, go back to when you first met and you two became friends. Back then you talked about any and every subject, from home to finances to food; when you didn't have money to buy food, think about how you shared, how you laughed, how you giggled, and how you had a great time together. There was no such thing as putting a lock on your phone. You could talk and you could see each other's phones. You could spend time together. Quality time.

But what happened? We allowed those saboteurs to come in and start causing issues. I'm going to use the analogy of a cup. The saboteur is like salt. You have a cup and you throw salt into the cup. And once you taste the salt, you have given the saboteur freedom to inquire, to ask questions about what's going on. You open up the pathway. See, the saboteur never would have realized what was going on in their marriage or their relationship until it was revealed and the knowledge was given to the saboteur. Then, the issue changed. It's like critical abandonment. What do you need to throw away in your home? What clothes are you holding on to? That high school jersey that you're never going to wear (you'll never be that player again!)? Just take a picture of it and remove it.

We're holding on to relationships but the relationships are over and done with. They'll never come back together. However, we allow those to sabotage our future relationships. How can a past relationship sabotage your future? Well, they've moved on. But when you're trying to accomplish your goals and dreams, the saboteur comes back and blocks them. It causes us to have stress. And stress and fear cause uneasiness. And uneasiness causes us to be uncomfortable. And being uncomfortable prevents us from being able to focus and think as we should because of those sabotaging issues.

So when we look at procrastination, decision, and fear, we can see how procrastination plus decision equals fear. But fear of what? Fear of having a great relationship. However, what if this relationship does turn out to be something good? Well, when we think about sabotage, we must get out of our minds what people think about us. There's always going to be somebody who doesn't like something that you're doing or who disagrees with work you're doing, or someone who doesn't like your proposal. Somebody is not going to like what you suggest in the meeting, is not going to like what you wear to the meeting, and is not going to like your ideas. But these are *your* ideas, to your greatness.

So when you look at critical issues and critical abandonment, what are some goals that you have? I often ask that question about goals and dreams. Are they real? Do they happen? Well, if you think about it, just imagine the captain of a ship. The captain's trying to take you on a journey and the journey's going to be thousands of miles across the Pacific Ocean. But imagine, the captain has to chart it, look at the weather, and look at the weather forecast seven to fifteen days ahead. He has to check his crew to see if they are adequately prepared for any trauma (medical or non-medical), that there is adequate food, and he must check whatever's going aboard his ship or his vessel. He has a goal. And he sticks to his goal and he lives by his goal.

Now, imagine another captain who makes the same trip. But this captain doesn't check the weather and he doesn't check with his crew about making sure they're prepared. This captain doesn't do a forecast. Who would you go with?

See, when we look at our lives, we let uncharted, unguided maps and individuals come into our lives and they cause critical abandonment. They cause us not to be able to remove the obstacles from our lives. Critical abandonment can be at your job. People might sit by you at your job and sabotage your thinking. They steal your time and they keep you from doing those things that you know are critical or crucial and have a deadline.

So, a lot of times you have to think about what you want. Who's sabotaging you? Remember, the saboteur was uninvited and you opened the door and let them in. We live in a conflicted society where so many things in our lives that we hold on to need to be eliminated. There are lots of things around our homes, like a picture or book, that bring us negative memories when we look at them. That's a saboteur. Remove it.

I'm always asked, well, what about somebody in my family? Remove them out of your psyche, remove them out of your life. If a person or thing is causing you problems, pain, imperfection, prevents you from being able to make a decision, or makes you uncomfortable or uneasy, they're a saboteur.

Moreover, saboteurs don't mind being saboteurs. Because if you look at a saboteur's life and the things in their lives — how they've lived, the jobs they've had, the way they dress, the way they carry themselves — you'll see that they are a fake model. They sabotage. They make you uncomfortable.

Look at your goals. Look at five of your friends right now. If you're overweight, there's a likelihood that your five friends are overweight. If you have a business that's not making the type of profits it should be making, look at your friends who have businesses. Theirs are probably just like yours.

What do we do? We hit critical mass. We change who we hang around with. We need to model a business or get a mentor, someone that's going to guide us in the direction that we want to go, and we're going to take what they're doing and model it — almost copy it — to achieve success.

I mentioned before that we are what we think about. We are what we see. The mind is 95 percent visual and it snaps pictures of what we're doing all day long. What visuals or pictures is your mind snapping that you want to model? A lot of success can be duplicated. But because of critical abandonment, we're prevented from accomplishing what's important to us. It can be business or it can be personal goals. There's nothing, business-wise or personally, that you can't achieve with great success if you set your mind to it. Go back to that.

Some goals and dreams are attainable that you didn't believe were possible until they happened. And sometimes, we have to surround ourselves with individuals who believe in us more than we believe in ourselves to see things come to fruition. They're able to see the critical abandonment, the obstacles that are blocking you from success. And whatever your success goal is, it's amazing. We sit down and talk to people about all the things going on in their lives, what they want to accomplish, what they want to do, what they want to dream, and it's hard to realize that a lot of people don't have a roadmap. They're stuck in a situation in life. And in life, we have choices. But sometimes, we only stop at the third attempt of trying to do something great because these choices can be painful.

You know, we're often told that it takes 21 days to make a change, meaning that when we look at making changes in our life, especially for the mind, body, and spirit, it takes approximately 21 days before we notice the change happening. But I'm here to tell you it takes about six weeks for the body and the mind to understand change.

Think about Thomas Edison, who had not much schooling at all. His parents and everyone around him thought he was a loser but he had the vision of creating a light bulb. He made over a thousand attempts to create the light bulb. Was it a failure? No, to him it was a thousand failures toward his success. But in our lives, we get to three and we stop. I can't write the book — it's too complicated, I don't have time, and my friend told me I'm wasting my time. Or my job is pulling me away from my writing. I can't lose weight because I can't stop eating. I can't change what I'm doing. I can't love my wife and I can't get into the relationship because of critical abandonment. Someone's always stopping you from doing those things that you want to do.

We live in a selfish society where we have so many useless things in our lives that we hold on to, and that should be eliminated. The goals that you have are *your* goals, *your* dreams, and *your* aspirations. I always asked these questions: Who are you uplifting today? Whose life do you want to help improve? You sit there and you say, okay, I want to make something happen. I want to get more clients. But who are you serving? Because it's not about you, it's about your clients. And when we realize that we are accountable to the client, all of a sudden it becomes a customer or client relationship that we're serving. We're making the customer happy. They're getting what they want and we're creating a solution.

What do you want? What are those critical abandonments in your life? As you look in the mirror, look around. Jot down the distractions that are stopping you from obtaining success. Who is it? What is it that's critical and a major situation? Because as we look at our lives, there's so much clutter — critical abandonment and clutter to the degree that we can't get through the cornfield because of the weeds. And the weeds are not really there, they're just clutter. And then we stop our journey to ask a saboteur what they think, what their ideal situation for *your* dream is. But it's *your* dream! It's *your* aspiration!

At 64 years old, Colonel Sanders decided to ask somebody about his chicken recipe and the person told him it wasn't going to work. What if they didn't like chicken? What if they wanted to be a beef eater? But Colonel Sanders, at 64, decided to go with his dream. The rest is history. It's amazing. Dr. Myles Monroe, a great man, a great visionary, and a great leader of God was asked about the rich people in the world. And Myles Monroe said that some of the richest minds, the richest dreams, and the richest people in the world are in the graveyard. They died with their dreams, their aspirations, and their goals. They either never told anybody or they were told that something wouldn't work, so they believed it and never tried.

If you think about it, who or what are you allowing to deny your happiness? Is it a spouse? Is it a friend? Is it a partner? Sometimes, we have to remove critical abandonment from our lives because it's starving us and preventing us from grabbing that gravitational greatness that we need.

It's amazing how children are so smart. They can play together, doesn't matter what race, creed, color at all. But what happens as they start to grow from a baby up? Critical abandonment sets in from negative and environmental issues. And all of a sudden, they change.

Look at where you are, look at your circumstances, and look at the people you work with every day. I'm amazed by how much critical abandonment we listen to every day in our automobiles going to work. Studies have shown that riding in your car a minimum of three to four hours per day is enough time to have a college degree at the end of the year. But consider what you listen to every day in your car. Music, talk radio...all of which you can listen to every once in a while but when you're trying to change, you have to involve your mentors. You have to put in motivational things. You have to put in something you're trying to learn to make the most of that valuable time.

And you might say, "Well, I have heard it all already." That's all right, your mind, your consciousness, is very powerful. A lot of things you think you're missing, the mind is picking them up. That's why we do repetition. We keep on listening to something over and over and over again until it becomes part of our psyche, like a song that you know. You didn't learn it the first time you heard it; you kept listening to it. The same applies to your greatness. Who are you listening to in order to change your life? What's holding you back from your success? And *who's* holding you back from your success?

What is on your mind to accomplish when you wake up in the morning? Is it just a job? Do you think, *I'm going to my job today? I've got to earn an income.* Why don't you change that to, *I'm going to MY company*? It's not just your job. And what can you do on that job individually, whether you work for someone or yourself, to make it a great day?

You are your ideas, your thoughts, and your dreams. You're asking questions. What is that beacon of light that's going to make you shine? Remember, the saboteurs are watching. The saboteurs stop you from trying to do things. *This is a company, it's not your company. You don't do this...* and *This is the boss.*

Why are you trying to make your company better? Because at that moment, that is what you're doing when you learn to give 120 percent of your time to somebody else. Then your greatness starts to shine.

We're always going to have haters. We're always going to have people who don't like us. These are the saboteurs in our lives. What are you going to do? Take a look at your life today. Take a hard look in the mirror and say, "I'm tired of not having the finances I want. I'm tired of not having the bank account I want. I'm tired of not having the peace that I want. I'm tired of not having the joy that I want. I'm tired of not having the vacations and the free time that I want. I'm going to start living for me!"

When it becomes about you for a moment, you learn how to relax and enjoy *you.* You're then able to become a better servant. If you remember every day, *Who can I serve today? Whose life can I improve today?* Guess what? Your life will improve automatically.

So, when you think about the dilemmas, the problems, and the situations that seem to be an issue, look at the saboteurs at work in your time, space, and energy. The question is, who or what are your saboteurs? It can be a person, place, or thing that is stopping you from doing those things that are causing critical abandonment in your life now.

Write down the top 20 and start eliminating them from your life today. Eliminate critical abandonment and saboteurs, regain control of your life, and live today as never before, starting now!

Your Thoughts

CHAPTER 6

GOALS

Our goals can only be reached through a vehicle of a plan, in which we must fervently believe, and upon which we must vigorously act. There is no other route to success.

— Pablo Picasso

Today, we're going to talk about goals, goals, and goals. It's amazing how goals work in our lives and sometimes, as we try to do things, how goals get in the way. Do you have goals set?

One of the main things I want to discuss in this book is having goals, things we're doing that are related to goals, and how we get in our own way as we try to accomplish those goals. When we write out our goals, we're supposed to write them out with the idea that we're going to look at them daily and understand that they're for ourselves and not anyone else. A lot of times with goals, we look at other people's lives and try to pattern our own lives, circumstances, or situations around them, which actually messes us up.

When you look at goals, you look at decisions, you look at life, and you look at what you're trying to do for yourself. You realize that everybody's goals are different. We read so many different books about goals and paradigm shifts, about what you should be doing and what you should not be doing. And at the end of the day, even as you're reading this, you might be thinking about it. What goals have I set for myself that I'm supposed to change or that are going to change me and make me a better person?

As you honestly look at your goals, are you where you want to be in life? Look at yourself in the mirror for a second. What makes you happy? What gives you joy? What gets you up in the morning? What drives your spirit when you look at what you're trying to accomplish? Have you accomplished it? Have you looked at your goals over and over and over again?

A lot of times, as we look at our goals, we realize that we are sometimes stuck in a situation where it seems like the more we plan, the more we think about it, the deeper we get into a situation where nothing comes to fruition in our lives. Our goals, our dreams, our aspirations — nothing comes to fruition!

What are we going to do? What do you want to do? What do you want to do with yourself? One of the questions I always ask my audience is, "When you look at yourself in the mirror, who do you see? What type of person do you see? Is that a person you really want to be?"

Look at yourself in the mirror and say, "I want to change" or "I want to make better goals. I want to do better in life." What does that really mean?

What is really stopping you from doing those things that you truly want to do? Well, I say, who's stopping you? How are you letting them stop you from doing those things? And why are you letting them stop you from doing those things that you know you should be doing daily? You will know when you think about it for a second.

When I read the book *Think and Grow Rich* by Napoleon Hill, I learned that you either walk at somebody else's pace or they're going to walk at your pace. And most of the time, we're going to pattern ourselves and walk at somebody else's pace and it's going to slow us down because you have to realize that nobody's dream is your dream.

The book *Conform* talks about chasing other people's dreams. Are we conforming to somebody else? Or are we trying to conform to ourselves? I want you to examine yourself for a second as you're reading and considering this. Stop and just examine it. What is it that you envision yourself to be? Now, go back and think about this for a second. As you grew up and as you came into yourself, what did you envision your life to be like at this point?

Now, I want you to stop and just really think about it. As you envision your life, what were you supposed to be doing at this point in your life? What has stopped you from being the way you wanted to be at this point in your life and how did you allow it to stop you? You have to really examine yourself for a second because this is a book about procrastinating; it's a book about changing the individual.

We read so many topics and so many headlines that say don't do this, don't do that. The question is, what do you want to do? What makes you happy? What gives you joy? What gives you life? What is it that you really want to do? We are always talking about other people. Ask yourself, "Well, what do I want to do?"

When you look at goals, who do you want to serve today?

What is the goal when you're asking somebody, "What do you need?" Think about it. "What do you need?" Has anybody asked you that?

Look in the mirror and ask yourself, "What do I need? What is going to make me happy? What's going to give me joy? What's going to help me love my children, my family, my wife, and my surroundings more? What do I need to do to change the things that I'm doing or following now?" Those are loaded questions when you look at it but they're real.

Write down three personal goals and three business goals. We need goals to function and live. We need a roadmap. Let me get you on the right track. Goals are dreams, aspirations, and roadmaps to get us to a point where we need to be and we keep living by those goals and dreams. But when you think about it, when you ask people, "What are your goals? What do you want to do? What makes you happy?"...you will get an array of answers. Some of those answers are just off the tops of their heads but when you think about it, if you sit and say, "I'm going to make a goal. I'm going to make a dream. I'm going to make a reality," what does it *really* mean?

Pause, stop reading, look around, and ask yourself, "Am I happy with my life?" Look at your life right now and determine how to improve it.

You might have set some goals for yourself this year. Are you on track for accomplishing those goals? There are multiple goals that we deal with every day but are you on track for this year's goals, not last year's? Sometimes that goal is just making that phone call — that phone call you thought you'd worry about later.

But sometimes, we have to remove the fear out of our anatomy, our stomach, and just make the call knowing that they're going to say one of two words: yes or no. Like you or not. Book me or don't book me. Let's meet or let's not meet.

What is it about fear that stops you from doing the things you should be doing? Goals! Have you sat and thought about them? What's the goal that you have for yourself weekly, monthly, daily? What is your life goal? What's that goal that you dream about and you're not doing? Who's stopping you? And why are you allowing them to stop you? What do you really need to be doing today that you're not doing to get your joy? Who's stopping you?

Just think about the time, whatever your age is, from 18 to now, what is it that you always wanted to achieve? And you might be 18 or 100 but just think about it — what do you reflect upon? And I'm often thinking about Dr. Myles Munroe when he talks about the richest place in the world. You know that the richest place in the world has more money than you can imagine. And he's talked about it multiple times, and a lot of times we don't realize it, but like he said, the richest place in the world is a graveyard. There are lots of goals that never came to fruition because people allowed other people, situations, and circumstances to stop them from doing the things that they needed to do or wanted to do — usually because someone said they couldn't do it.

Are you in that spot today? Someone's telling you that you can't do something? Who's negative or what's negative in your life that you're allowing to control your life, your goals, and your dreams? You know, when we think about goals, we should also think about people that are not for us. I often think about the people I've talked to in my life. I remember a person named Jay, and I was talking to Jay about what I was planning to do in the future. I said, "Jay, I'm going to be a motivational speaker. I'm gonna travel all over the country, but Jay, I'm going to do certain things with my life and I'm gonna be wealthy."

And the first thing Jay said to me was, "How are you gonna do that?"

And I said, "I'm just gonna do it. I'm gonna study, I'm gonna read books, I'm gonna talk to mentors, and I'm gonna go to workshops. I'm gonna do the things that I need to do to change my outlook."

And all Jay could say was, "That's gonna cost money. You can't do that. That's gonna cost more time than you've got. Who's gonna help you? Why do you think you're gonna be able to do it?"

Do you have a Jay in your life? Jays are everywhere. Jay is not just a guy; Jay is a girl, an individual. Jay is a family member, people in your life, or coworkers. It could be workers, the boss, the supervisors, and everybody around you who is a Jay. But remember, this dream, this goal that you're talking about — it's about you. It's not about anybody but you. It's about you encompassing every aspect of your life and doing the things that you really want to do.

Think about your goals. Write them down. What is the income that you want right now for yourself? And what are your expenses right now? Because a lot of times, you don't make plans for income expansion, though we look at assets and capital. I want you to think about this goal for a minute. What income do you want to make?

So, you have to put all the goals and dreams together but you have to consider income and expenses as well. Then you take those two and you divide them — the desired income that you want by your expenses. Then you have what your outlay should be. Now the question is, are you going to pursue those goals? Are you going to write them out? Are you going to make a habit of looking at your goals every day, two or three times a day? Are you going to make a habit of writing down your goals every morning; what you need to accomplish that day? If not, why? Who's stopping you?

Why are you afraid? What makes you so uncomfortable when you think about it? When we talk about procrastinating, we ask, "Why are we afraid of success?"

What if success is stopping you from reaching your goals and your dreams? Is it a co-worker? Is it really? Or is it that you just don't believe in yourself? You know, it could be that we just don't believe in ourselves as we should. We let "self" stop us from a lot of stuff. *Why should it happen to me? Who am I?* Who are you? You are great at what you're doing. You can do anything you set your mind to, but a lot of times it's a paradigm shift.

We can't envision it. Sometimes it seems impossible but a lot of times, you have to get away from everybody who is negative and as a result, you might not have a lot of friends. You're going to have a short string of friends. So if you're trying to be friends with everybody, let's stop, right this moment. Because if you've got a lot of friends and you're trying to make everybody happy, one thing is for sure: you're going to be broke. You're not going to make any money, you're not going to be happy, and you're going to live a miserable life. You might get by with certain things but that life that you're trying to get, the life you're trying to have, you'll never have.

First, you've got to decide: What are you going to do? Look at the man in the mirror. Quit blaming your circumstances. Quit blaming all the dreams and goals that you had planned that aren't happening, and quit blaming other individuals because those individuals have nothing to do with *your* dreams.

You know, think about it! How does a person like Donald Trump make the money he makes? How does a person like Elon Musk make the money he makes? How does a person like Jay Abraham, the world-renowned Internet marketing specialist and business advisor, make the money he makes? How do you make the money you make? When you think about the people all around us making millions and billions of dollars, what is different between them and you? Goals, dreams, aspiration, and sweat. Some of them don't get much sleep because they are working on their dreams, goals, and their aspirations.

A lot of times, we just don't do it. We just want it to happen. We just want to walk through the door. We lay everything out and nothing happens or we don't do anything that's going to permeate our lives because it's a change. And change is scary. We stop a project after numerous no's and we put the project aside and say, "It doesn't work."

Just imagine for a minute when Thomas Edison tried 1,069

times to create the light bulb. What if he had stopped at 1,068 times? The light bulb would never have been invented. (It likely would have eventually but we don't know.) What if he had just stopped? What is it that you're not willing to put the time into, that you're not willing to put the effort into? What is it that you're not willing to put the sweat equity into? What is stopping you? Who's stopping you?

Write down on your piece of paper: My number-one goal today is...what? My number-two goal today is...what? My number-three goal today is...what? My number-four goal today is...what?

Now, as you write out these goals, you have to believe in them. You have to put them into your mind and soul. You have to say, "I'm gonna make this happen."

One thing about goals that successful people do is they read their goals for *today*...but they also read their goals for *tomorrow*.

Now, you might say, "Why?"

It's like envisioning making a sale. Have you ever said, "I'm gonna make a presentation tomorrow," but the night before you make that presentation, you practice in your mind? You need to have positive energy. Energy is the key because if you don't have any energy, your audience is going to see that you have no energy.

You must have energy so that before you ever make the presentation, you envision that you've already made the sale. You can see that you've already made a successful speech. You can see you've already made someone happy in the audience. You can see it! And if you see it before you ever deliver it, it's already accomplished. How many times have you done that? Your vision is powerful! Then, when you actually make the presentation or you talk to the individual, the company, or the people about it, everybody's in-tune with it and says, "Ah!" And you are successful.

That's the way life is sometimes. It throws us through those kinds of curves that we're not prepared for. When you think about your goals, what are they? Let's quit living in somebody else's dream. What are your goals? What is it going to take today for you to turn your life around?

It's amazing when we think about goals and we think about why we can't make any money...oh, nobody's hiring me! Why don't you get a job? Why don't you create revenue every day for yourself and quit procrastinating? Stop doing what people want you to do. Do what makes you happy. Do what gives you joy! What is that? When's the last time you just took a ride in your automobile, on a train, or on a bus down the road to nowhere, and just thought about what your life should be like? Not what it *is*, what it *should be?* When are you going to believe in yourself? When are you going to believe in what you've got inside of you? When are you going to trust yourself? Ah, that's a major issue! A lot of times, we don't trust the individual staring back at us in the mirror — and that's us! Why don't we trust ourselves?

What is it that makes us fearful? You weren't born with fear. One thing about goals is, when you talk to people about them, they have fears. "Oh, I have goals," you might say. I talk to individuals every day who say this.

"Can you tell me about your goals? What do you want to

do?" I ask them. And they're so broad or so short or so long that they're unreachable. You've got to believe in them because once you write your goals out, your mind believes it and can see it, and knows the reality that this is something that you're trying to do. And one thing about it is, it happens! It comes off the paper!

What do you want? You know you procrastinate, we all do, but how do you want to start the process of change? Write down your goals. What are your aspirations? Close your eyes and think about the things that you really want to do for yourself. If you're married, it might be something for your family or your children. What do you really want to do? Then go back. What do you want to change? Can you write the name of the individual that you really want to get away from on that goal sheet? Who do you want to be? This is for you, not for another individual that you want to pattern yourself after. *It's for you!*

What do you want to be? Who do you want to be? What do you want to look like? Where do you envision yourself in five years, 10 years, 20 years, 30 years, or 100 years from now?

You need to look at your goals, dreams, and aspirations, and if your circumstances or situations are not where you want them to be, it's time! It's time to change your mindset. The mind is so powerful and it can create your failures or your successes. The choice is yours.

We think about many different things but we don't use half of the capacity of our minds trying to actualize our plans. You only use about five percent of your brain. Can you imagine if you could use 25 percent of your mind today? Oh, my God!

How much power would you have? Think of the things you could accomplish! But guess what? With the mindset you have now, you can't accomplish them. You have to believe what you're doing because this dream is yours. It's not your neighbor's, it's not your family member's, it's not your co-worker's, and it's not your spouse's; it's *your* dream.

It's almost like when you think about your children (if you have children) and you say, "That's my namesake." The kid looks like you, talks like you, and walks like you. And you say, "Wow, he's a duplicate of me!" But is he really? What are the dreams you envision for your children? Are you teaching your children how to dream at a young age? Are you teaching your children how to set goals? Are you instilling things in their minds that actually make them become a better person than you? That's one of the hardest things. Do you want them to be better than you? Yes!

As you reflect on this and you think about what your goals are, what your dreams are, what your aspirations are, I challenge you to write down your goals. What are your goals? Then also, who are you? What do you want to be like? When you're writing out who you want to be, have you ever thought about that person? Who that person really is? You can think about the money you want to make every day, you can write everything down in goals and dreams and aspirations to a point. But then you've got to *believe it*. You've got to feel it in your soul, where your dreams are a part of you and you know that, "I am becoming that individual," or, "I have become that person."

Your goals should start to become a daily part of your life.

What do you wake up in the morning listening to as you're putting your goals, dreams, and aspirations together? Who you listen to determines your outlook for the day because so much negative information comes to us on a daily basis. Who do you listen to? And then you need to pattern yourself. You have to be accountable for your goals, your dreams, and aspirations to an individual, a mentor, a coach, or somebody that you can work with. But this individual has to already be the way you want to be and beyond.

Stop patterning yourself, your dreams, and your goals after folks that are not going anywhere. Now, what I mean by *anywhere* is, they're not making the money that you want to make or they don't have the habits that you want to have. They're just functioning.

Think about it. Goals, finances, expenses...what does my life need to be like and what am I going to do to create revenue every day?

Creating revenue every day should be your goal. That's part of what this book is all about. However, procrastination is reducing your revenue and happiness every day.

Let's talk about these goals. Write them out. Then stop! Put a big old stop sign there, and say, "Am I accomplishing these goals?"

If you're not, sit back down and let's look at how to make these goals come to fruition and help you to be the person you want to be, starting today. Are you preventing your own success? Look in the mirror. What is your number-one goal?

Your Thoughts

CONCLUSION

Sometimes we find ourselves returning to a task repeatedly, still unwilling to take the first step. We hear a little voice in our head saying, "Yeah, good idea, but...no." At this point, we need to ask that voice some questions to figure out what's really making it unappealing to take action. Patiently ask yourself a few "why" questions — "Why does it feel tough to do this?" "Why am I not motivated?"— and you'll find that the blockage will surface quite quickly.

Often, the issue is that a perfectly valid competing commitment is undermining your motivation. For example, suppose you were finding it hard to stick to an early morning goal-setting routine. A few "whys" might highlight that the challenge stems from your equally strong desire to eat breakfast with your family.

Once you've made that conflict more apparent, it's far more likely you'll find a way to overcome it; perhaps by setting your daily goals the night before or during your commute to work.

So, the next time you find yourself mystified by your inability to get important tasks done, be kind to yourself. Recognize that your brain needs help if it's going to be less short-sighted. Try taking at least one step to make the benefits of action loom larger, and one to make the costs of action feel smaller. Your languishing to-do list will thank you!

About the Author

Dr. Timothy K. Moore is an international motivational speaker and eight-times best-selling author, lecturer, educator, and business consultant. Traveling extensively throughout the world, Dr. Moore addresses crucial issues affecting individuals' social, spiritual, and business development and helps them work toward the goal of transforming their lives.

Contact Information

EMAIL
support@writingbestsellers.com
gmresourcegroup@gmail.com

Publisher: gmresourcegroup

Link to talk:
https://growingyourbusiness.as.me/?appointmentType=34327
92

When you're ready for improvement, let's talk!